WATERLOO TO WINDSOR

Vic Mitchell and Keith Smith

Cover picture: The "Windsor" side of Water-loo station on 1st April 1933 includes 3-coach suburban unit no. 1785 and ex-SECR class F1 4–4–0 no. 1074, bound for Reading.
(H.C. Casserley)

Design – Deborah Goodridge

First published July 1988

ISBN 0 906520 54 1

© Middleton Press, 1988

Typeset by CitySet - Bosham 573270

Published by Middleton Press
        Easebourne Lane
        Midhurst, West Sussex
        GU29 9AZ
        ☎ (073 081) 3169

Printed & bound by Biddles Ltd,
        Guildford and Kings Lynn

CONTENTS

MAPS

ACKNOWLEDGEMENTS

We are very grateful to the many photographers mentioned in the captions for help received and also to J.H. Aston, P. Hay, F.W. Ivey, J.R.W. Kirkby, A.C. Mott, R. Randell, D. Salter, E. Staff, N. Stanyon, R. Stevenson and our ever helpful wives. We again thank Mrs. M. Mason and Mr. D. Wallis for the use of photographs taken by the late E. Wallis and as always are pleased to have received tickets from the collections of G. Croughton and N. Langridge.

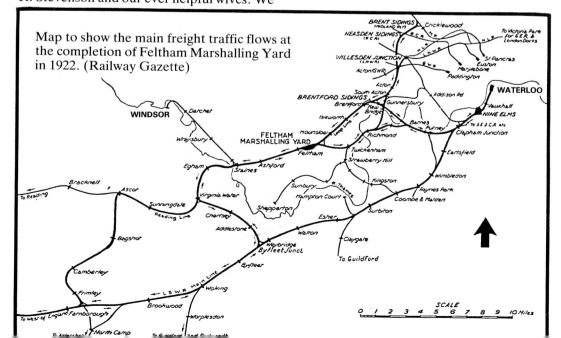

Map to show the main freight traffic flows at the completion of Feltham Marshalling Yard in 1922. (Railway Gazette)

GEOGRAPHICAL SETTING

The entire route is set in the Thames Valley. From Waterloo to Richmond it runs south of the river and crosses two small tributaries – the River Wandle, west of Wandsworth Town, and the Beverley Brook, west of Barnes. After crossing the River Thames beyond Richmond, it passes over the River Crane (twice) and the River Colne (in Staines). The parallel Colne Brook is bridged adjacent to Wraysbury station and the final river crossing is on the approach to Windsor, where the line regains the south bank.

Remarkably level, the route reaches the 50ft. contours near Feltham and reaches a maximum altitude of a mere 70ft. above sea level at Windsor. The town is strategically situated on an isolated and prominent outcrop of chalk in a broad band of London Clay which extends from the metropolis. The entire route traverses this clay, on which gravels are found west of Feltham. These have been of some economic importance to the railway in times past.

HISTORICAL BACKGROUND

The London & Southampton Railway's first length of line was between London (Nine Elms) and Woking (Common) and came into use on 21st May 1838. A branch from it to Richmond was opened on 27th July 1846, quadruple track being provided from the terminus to the point of divergence. The lines were extended to Waterloo (Bridge) on 11th July 1848 and to Datchet on 22nd August 1848.

Queen Victoria gave consent for the London & South Western Railway to extend their line from Datchet, across Home Park, to within the shadow of Windsor Castle. This extension opened on 1st December 1849, only a few weeks after the GWR branch reached the town. Both companies had been required to pay vast sums of money "towards local improvements", for the privilege of entering the then railway resistant town.

1850 saw the completion of the Hounslow loop line and, in 1856, the Staines to Ascot branch came into use.

The West London Extension Railway was opened on 2nd March 1863 to Kensington, to link with the 1844 branch from the LNWR main line. The railway was owned jointly by the GWR (⅓), the LNWR (⅓), the LBSCR (⅙) and the LSWR (⅙). Clapham Junction station and numerous connecting lines were built at that time at the southern end of the line.

A branch from Twickenham to Kingston was opened on 1st July 1863, the Kingston loop being completed in 1869. The LSWR commenced running north from Richmond to Kensington (Addison Road, later Olympia) via Turnham Green and Hammersmith (Grove Road) on 1st January 1869. Part of this branch was used by Metropolitan District trains from 1877. North London trains used it from the outset, having earlier reversed at Old Kew Junction *and* Barnes to reach Richmond. (Some trains ran on to Twickenham and Kingston at that time.)

A joint LSWR/Metropolitan District line between Wimbledon and Putney Bridge was opened on 3rd June 1889, although LSWR trains did not cross the bridge but took the curve to Point Pleasant Junction to reach Waterloo.

The first electric services on the LSWR commenced on 20th October 1915 and operated between Waterloo and Wimbledon, via East Putney. Electrification of the Hounslow and Kingston loops followed in 1916 with regular electric services commencing to Windsor on 6th July 1930.

PASSENGER SERVICES

The initial service to Datchet was of eight trains daily, although there were two less on Sundays. By 1869, there were 12 trains each way on weekdays and 5 on Sundays. This had increased to 21 and 7 respectively in 1910, with four additional weekday trains between Windsor and Woking or beyond. These used the spur at Staines, thus avoiding Staines Junction. An interesting experiment in through running took place in 1854 when three trains per day were run between Broad Street and Windsor, via Acton, Brentford and Staines.

In the 1920s, a regular interval hourly weekday service was introduced to Windsor and in the 1930s this was improved to 30 minute intervals, seven days a week. Additional trains from Reading and Aldershot have always augmented the service from Staines eastwards while the Hounslow and Kingston loop lines have provided many extra local trains to Waterloo from the suburban areas. Since May 1987, most Hounslow line trains have run to Staines and have terminated alternately at Weybridge and Woking. The Kingston Loop services were withdrawn in May 1985, since when most trains from Waterloo via Twickenham have terminated at Kingston.

All maps in this album are to the scale of 25″ to 1 mile unless otherwise stated.

Map to show the two approaches to Kensington for trains from Richmond in the late nineteenth century. (Railway Magazine)

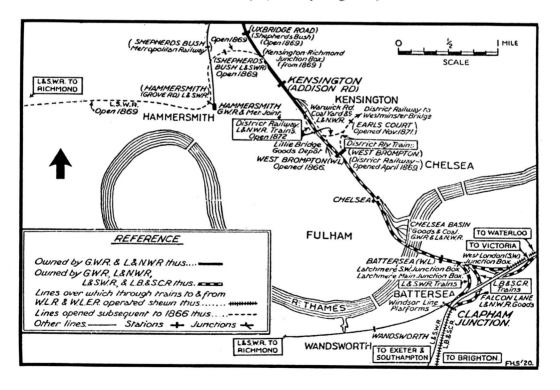

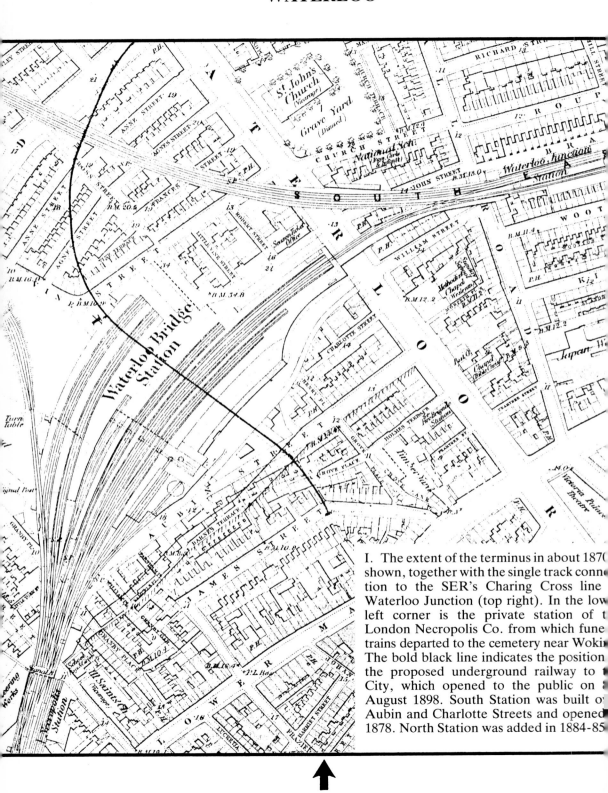

I. The extent of the terminus in about 1870 shown, together with the single track connection to the SER's Charing Cross line Waterloo Junction (top right). In the low left corner is the private station of the London Necropolis Co. from which funeral trains departed to the cemetery near Woking. The bold black line indicates the position the proposed underground railway to City, which opened to the public on August 1898. South Station was built over Aubin and Charlotte Streets and opened 1878. North Station was added in 1884-85.

1. Only North Station remains today, as platforms 16 to 21. Confusingly, pairs of platforms were originally given only one number – no. 9 is now 19 and 20. (Lens of Sutton)

2. The last 'A' Box was erected in 1892 and here we see the removal of the girders that supported its predecessor. On the left is the first Necropolis station, which was replaced in 1902 to allow for track widening. (Late E. Wallis collection)

3. 'A' Box remained in use until replaced by the present all electric box on 18th October 1936. There were 266 levers which could perform 410 functions by using the six gear levers. (Late E. Wallis collection)

4. The old composite station became the subject of music hall jokes, notably a well worn one about ghosts of passengers still trying to find the exit. The rebuilding took over twenty years and included the new offices and cab road seen here. (Lens of Sutton)

5. Class T9 no.724 arrives showing the headcode used for Reading via Twickenham after 21st June 1936. Prior to that, it was used for Hampton Court services. 'S' denotes shunt signals and arms resembling bow ties indicate "shunt wrong road". Until the late 1870s, incoming trains stopped at a ticket collecting platform west of Westminster Bridge Road; the locomotive was attached by means of a piece of rope which was released as the train approached the station. The engine was quickly diverted to a siding and the coaches ran into the platform, under the control of the guard. (D. Cullum collection)

6. The station suffered appalling bomb damage during World War II, the glass roof adding considerably to the hazard. This bomb failed to explode after passing through platform 2 on 24th September 1940. Graphic accounts of the period are to be found in *War on the Line*, reprinted by Middleton Press. (British Rail)

8. Class H16 4–6–2T no. 30519 departs with empty coaches for Clapham Yard on 26th March 1959, as cranes begin to change the London skyline. Further change is now imminent as plans show that all the buildings on the left of this view will be demolished to make way for the international railway terminus, the four platforms of which will extend to the right foreground of the picture. (J. Scrace)

7. Evidence of bomb damage remained in this 1948 photograph. The entrance arch had been dedicated as a memorial to railwaymen who lost their lives in WWI. This was the station's centenary year and around 95,000 passengers were arriving and departing daily. (NRM)

9. After the worst blizzard in living memory, men work to clear blocked and frozen points on 30th December 1962 as nos. 34071 and 34095 prepare for a difficult run. Lines to the south and west were blocked repeatedly as snow fell upon snow for weeks. (R.E. Ruffell)

10. Snow was still laying on 5th February 1963, as class M7 no. 30249 stood in the east wind which kept temperatures below freezing for almost three months – even the sea froze. These faithful locomotives handled most empty carriage movements until being largely ousted by ex-GWR Pannier 0–6–0Ts in 1959. (R.E. Ruffell)

11. North of the Windsor line platforms is the Armstrong lift which enables Waterloo & City line coaches to be hoisted to and from their underground habitat. It was photographed in August 1972, shortly before conversion from hydraulic (water) power operation to electricity. It is planned to retain the lift in the design of the international terminal. (R.E. Ruffell)

12. Three generations of electric stock stand in platforms 18, 17 and 16 on 29th December 1971 – 4COR no. 3126 (Guildford via Richmond), 4SUB no. 4291 (Kingston loop) and 4VEP no. 7814 (Reading via Richmond). The buffer stops of the proposed new platforms will be in the foreground of this picture, to allow for the creation of a larger concourse. Windsor line trains will be transferred to new platforms between nos. 11 & 12 (where the roadway is at present) and between platforms 15 & 16, at the end of the offices on the right. (R.E. Ruffell)

VAUXHALL

14. Opened on the same day as Waterloo, the station similarly had the suffix "Bridge" in its early years. By 1898, there were four pairs of tracks and in 1907 the "Up Windsor Through" reached Vauxhall. A down Guildford service approaches the station on 27th March 1909. (Ken Nunn collection/LCGB)

◄━━━━
13. 309 miniature levers were installed to control the approach to all 21 platforms. By 1948 the box was handling about 1200 train movements each day and forty years later it was reaching the end of its life. It is to be replaced by a panel located at Wimbledon. (R.E. Ruffell)

Other maps and photographs which help to tell the story of the development of this important terminus are contained in our *Waterloo to Woking* album.

15. After spending about half of its life on the Lyme Regis branch, 4–4–2T no. 30582 hauled the REC railtour to Windsor and other former LSWR stations on 19th March 1961. This 0415 class was introduced in 1882 for the Waterloo suburban services, which they commonly worked until electrification. (J. Scrace)

17. Viewed from the "Down Windsor" platforms, electro-diesel no. 73122 *County of East Sussex* (now renumbered 73207), hauls the empty royal train stock towards Waterloo, on 7th August 1985. The station was partly rebuilt in 1936, in connection with the new running arrangement following the opening of the Wimbledon flyover. (J. Scrace)

16. Once a good interchange point with the tramways, the station is now a convenient place for suburban passengers to change to the underground Victoria line. For decades, milk tankers stood in Platform 8 (behind the wall in the photograph) and discharged their contents into a bottling plant housed in one of the many brick arches supporting the track. (C. Hall)

SOUTHERN RAILWAY.
This Ticket is issued subject to the By-laws Regulations & Conditions stated in the Company's Time Tables Bills & Notices available on DAY of issue ONLY
WANDSWORTH TOWN to
Wandsworth Tn. Wandsworth Tn
Vauxhall Vauxhall
VAUXHALL
Third Class (S.1) Third Class
Fare ½d Fare 3½d

NINE ELMS

II. The 1895 edition shows the three pairs of tracks from Waterloo on the right and the original terminal building marked "Offices". The largest building in Brunswick Yard was a granary and the sidings in the top right of the map were used exclusively for manure. Cattle pens are to be found south of the brewery and no less than six sidings cross the street tramway on the level. South of the main line is part of the LSWR Locomotive Works, which was transferred to Eastleigh in 1909.

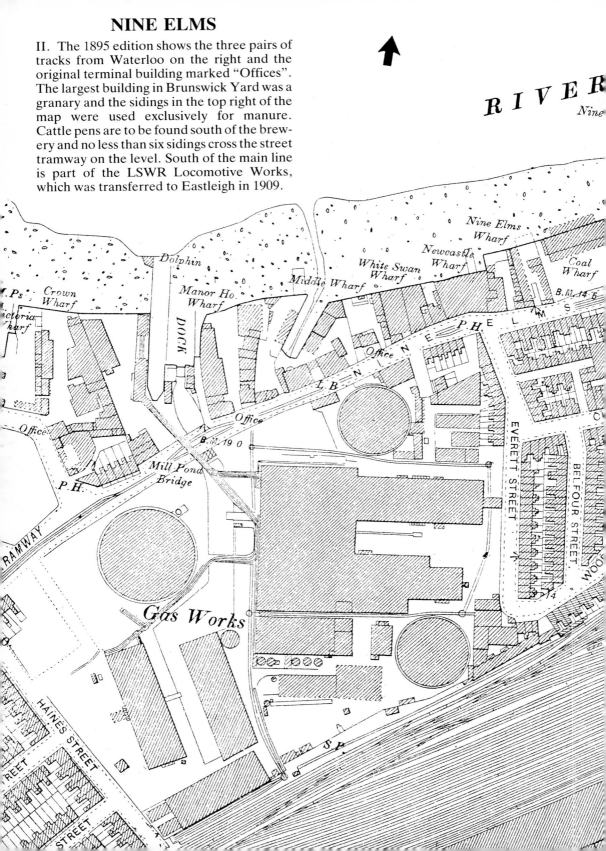

RIVER
Nine

Nine Elms Wharf

Newcastle Wharf

White Swan Wharf

Middle Wharf

Coal Wharf

B.M. 14·5

Dolphin

Crown Wharf

Manor Ho Wharf

Victoria Wharf

DOCK

Office

N E   P.H   E L S

L B N

Office

Office

B.M. 19·0

Mill Pond Bridge

P.H.

RAMWAY

EVERETT STREET

BELFOUR STREET

WOO

Gas Works

HAINES STREET

REET

STREET

S.P.

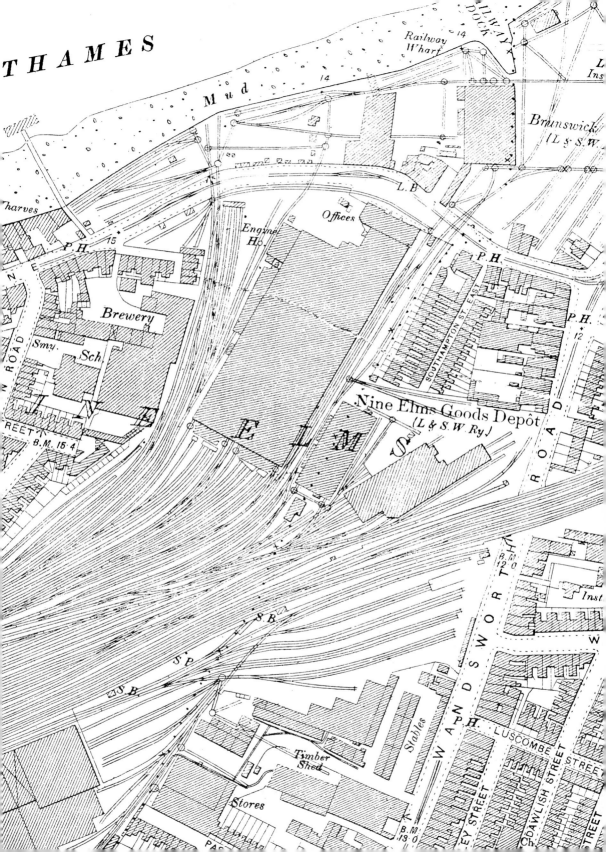

THAMES

Mud

Railway
Wharf

14

14

ILWAY
DOCK

L.
Ins

Railway Wharf

Brunswick
(L & S.W.

L.B

Offices

Engine
H.

harves

P.H.

15

P.H.

P.H.

P.H.

12

Brewery

Smy.

Sch.

ROAD

N E

SOUTHAMPTON ST EAST

Nine Elms Goods Depôt

(L & S.W. Ry.)

L I N E

STREET

B.M. 15.4

E L M S

ROAD

B.M.
12.0

Inst.

WANDSWORTH

W

S.B.

S.P.

S.B.

Stables

P.H.

LUSCOMBE STREET

Timber
Shed

EY STREET

DAWLISH STREET

STREET

Stores

B.M.
13.0

19. The former locomotive works became a goods depot (sheds H and J), a single track passing under the Waterloo lines to link the two depots. Wagons became derailed at the north end of this connection on 26th January 1963, probably due to packed snow.
(R.E. Ruffell)

18. Seen in about 1890, the handsome exterior makes interesting comparisons with the other terminal buildings at Southampton and Gosport, which still stand, at least in part. Other impressive out-of-town termini also became humble goods offices – for example Birmingham Curzon Street. (N.R.M.)

20. Nine Elms running shed was normally reached via this vacuum operated turntable on which Merchant Navy class no. 35016 *Elders Fyffes* is seen on 20th August 1963. Map IX in *Waterloo to Woking* shows its location. (R.E. Ruffell)

21. Passengers to Waterloo could not see this view, as the 15-road shed faced south. The transverse roof of the other 12-road shed can be seen on the right. Present on 20th August 1963 were representatives of classes U, N, S15, BR4 & 5 and all the Bulleid Pacifics.
(R.E. Ruffell)

22. Loco Junction Box was photographed shortly after its closure in June 1974, after the new Covent Garden Market had been built on the site of the former Locomotive Works and Depot, on the right. Lack of an effective national transport policy meant that no sidings were provided for fruit and vegetable traffic. Maybe this will be rectified if the proposed spur between the Windsor lines, on the left, and the Kent lines (which pass over a bridge behind the camera) is built for use by trains from mainland Europe.
(J. Scrace)

QUEENSTOWN ROAD

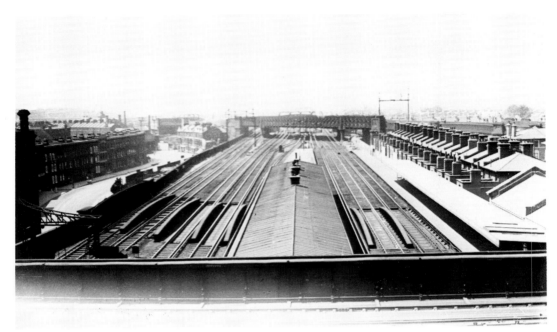

23. Looking west from the bridge carrying the South London Line from Victoria over the Waterloo lines in about 1932, we see the lattice structure which bears the quadruple tracks between Victoria and Clapham Junction. From right to left – Up Windsor Local; Nine Elms Goods Departure; Up Windsor Through; Down Windsor; Up Main Local; Up Main Through; Down Main Through and Down Main Local. (Late E. Wallis)

24. The station was opened as Queens Road Battersea on 1st November 1877, with a single island platform, the Up Local platform being added in 1909. Class M7 no. 30249 hauls the ex-North London Railway directors' saloon, followed by the ex-Midland and Glasgow & South Western Railways Joint Dining Saloon, from Nine Elms to Battersea Yard en route to Clapham Museum on 18th September 1959. (J.J. Smith)

25. A photograph from 14th April 1969 shows major reconstruction of the former LBSCR bridge. An alternative and earlier route between Victoria and Clapham Junction still exists, passing *under* the Waterloo lines, east of the station. (D. Cullum)

26. The exterior has recently been renovated and the original name exposed, although the station became Queenstown Road on 12th May 1980. The booking hall is no longer used as such, as the solitary member of staff issues and collects tickets on the island platform, where all local trains now call. (Lens of Sutton)

27. West London Junction Box straddles the four Windsor lines (left) and the four main lines for Woking trains. The original LBSCR route to Victoria dips away in the centre of the picture, while the 1867 elevated route curves to the right. The white house in the divergence was occupied for many years by the Battersea Borough Council Roads & Health Inspector. This and the next photograph were taken in 1957. (British Rail)

28. Looking west from West London Junction Box, the trackbed of the connection to the West London Line is evident, on the right, the line being just visible by the signals. Plans have been made to relay this spur for use by international trains that will reverse at Waterloo, to and from the north, east and west of Britain. The scheme also proposes use of the connection by empty stock to and from a new depot near North Pole Junction. The non-electrified lines in the centre of the picture lead to the carriage washing machine and Clapham Yard. On the left, a local train proceeds towards Victoria. (British Rail)

CLAPHAM JUNCTION

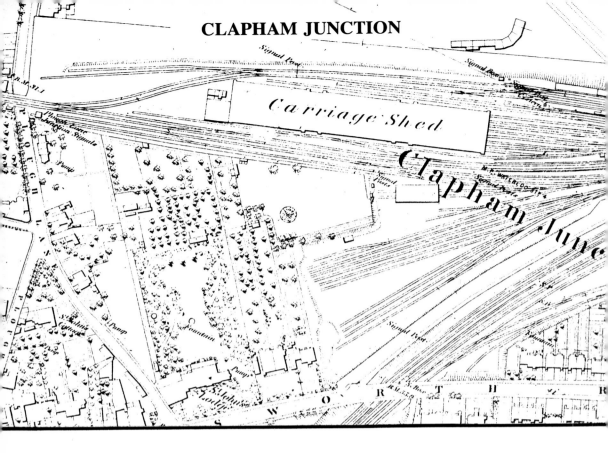

29. This poor quality photograph is worth including as it is the only one known to have been taken from the temporary East Box during the alterations in 1906. We look towards Waterloo – the West London connection diverges to the left. (Late E. Wallis collection)

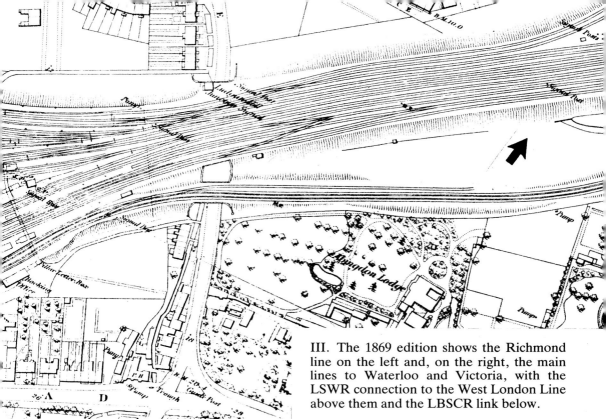

III. The 1869 edition shows the Richmond line on the left and, on the right, the main lines to Waterloo and Victoria, with the LSWR connection to the West London Line above them and the LBSCR link below.

30. A new box was erected across the Windsor Lines and brought into use on 4th February 1912. Initially called East Box, it became 'A' Box in 1924, and on 10th May 1965 suffered corrosion failure, dropping several feet at the north end. Major disruption to services ensued. (R.E. Ruffell)

31. Q1 class no. 33009, with its original number (C9) chalked onto its grimy cab side, passes under 'A' Box, five weeks after the collapse. The corrugated steel roofing, seen in the previous picture, had been added during WWII to deflect incendiary bombs. The assorted freight wagons are in transit from Nine Elms to Feltham. (R.E. Ruffell)

32. No. 33210 hauls the coaches of the Venice Simplon Orient Express on a private charter from Victoria to Middlesbrough, on 10th October 1986. The train will have crossed under the Waterloo lines twice and is just leaving the curve seen on the right of picture no. 28. (J. Scrace)

33. Like most of the signal boxes from Brookwood to Salisbury, West London Junction and Clapham Junction (West and East Boxes) were fitted with low pressure air operated signalling equipment. The line pressure was 15 p.s.i. and the signals and points operated at 7 p.s.i. This is the Windsor line frame in East Box in 1912.
(Late E. Wallis collection)

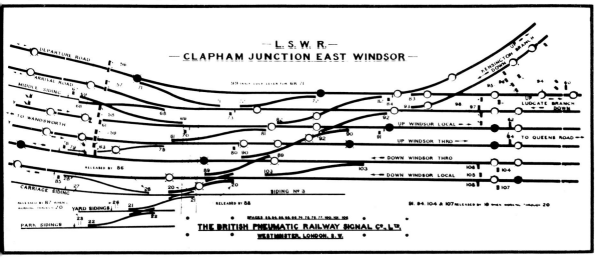

Other pictures, diagrams and maps are included in our *Victoria to East Croydon* and *Waterloo to Woking* volumes.

34. A view west from the footbridge above the down Windsor platforms in August 1956 includes some of the 52 carriage sidings. In addition, on the right are the seven "Kensington sidings", in which some milk tanks are stabled. An air cylinder is visible beside E Box (originally West Windsor), which was redesignated C Box in February 1957 and closed in November 1980. (D. Cullum)

35. Looking to the left of the previous picture and ten years later, we see the repair shed (on the right) which accommodates sidings 30-32 and part of the carriage shed in which sidings 7-12 are situated. Following the Bournemouth electrification scheme, sidings 9-13, 40 and 44-49 received conductor rails. (R.E. Ruffell)

36. Local trains to Kensington Olympia depart from platforms 2 or 16, in the business hours only. This is no. 33206 with the 08.12 from no. 2 on 19th August 1982. This little known service is mainly used by office workers and regrettably has not been expanded and publicised for the benefit of exhibition visitors. (J. Scrace)

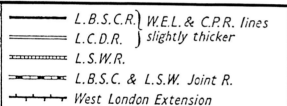

———————— L.B.S.C.R. ⎱ W.E.L. & C.P.R. lines
══════════ L.C.D.R. ⎰ slightly thicker
┅┅┅┅┅┅ L.S.W.R.
✕══✕══✕ L.B.S.C. & L.S.W. Joint R.
┼──┼──┼── West London Extension Joint Railway

IV. Diagram to show pre-grouping ownership of lines in the Clapham Junction area.

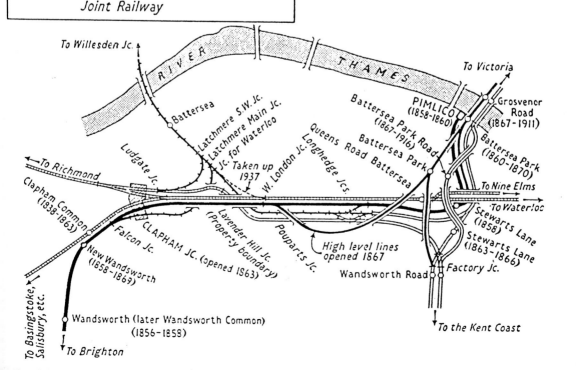

WANDSWORTH TOWN

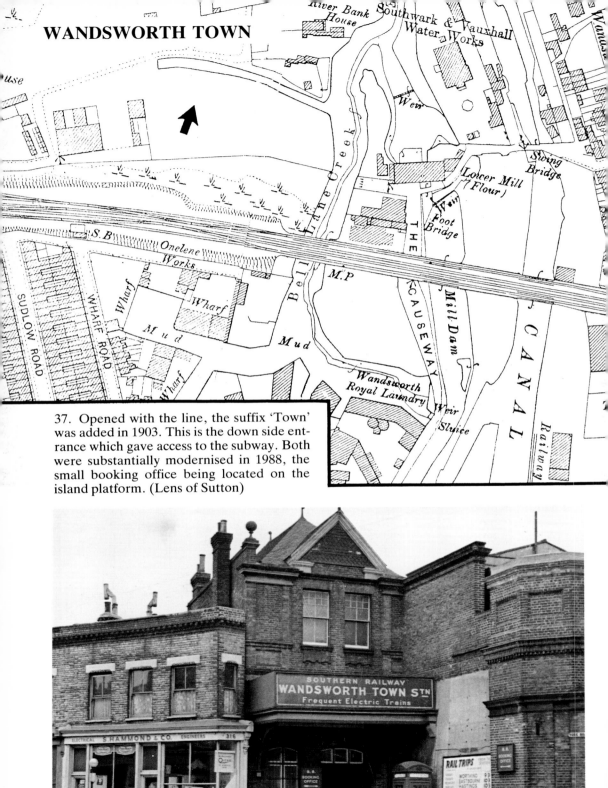

37. Opened with the line, the suffix 'Town' was added in 1903. This is the down side entrance which gave access to the subway. Both were substantially modernised in 1988, the small booking office being located on the island platform. (Lens of Sutton)

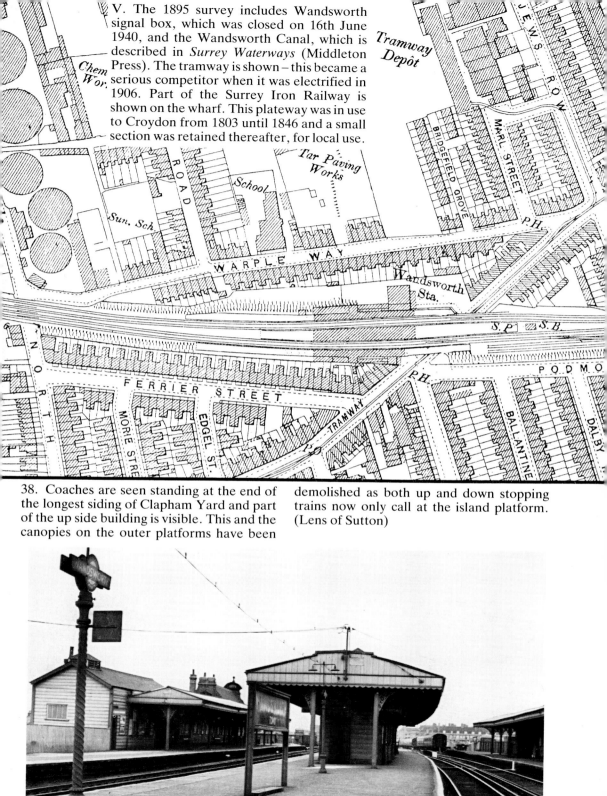

V. The 1895 survey includes Wandsworth signal box, which was closed on 16th June 1940, and the Wandsworth Canal, which is described in *Surrey Waterways* (Middleton Press). The tramway is shown – this became a serious competitor when it was electrified in 1906. Part of the Surrey Iron Railway is shown on the wharf. This plateway was in use to Croydon from 1803 until 1846 and a small section was retained thereafter, for local use.

38. Coaches are seen standing at the end of the longest siding of Clapham Yard and part of the up side building is visible. This and the canopies on the outer platforms have been demolished as both up and down stopping trains now only call at the island platform. (Lens of Sutton)

39. A train of milk tanks from Morden waits behind a Q1 class 0–6–0 on the Putney fly-over for an up train from Hounslow to clear Point Pleasant Junction on 12th August 1965. The down line to East Putney and Wimbledon is seen rising on the arches on the right. Thorleys and BP had sidings on the north side of the line, between the junction and the Wandle Viaduct. (R.E. Ruffell)

← 40. Looking from the other side of the brake van, the guard saw unit no. 5665 passing under Woodlands Bridge, with the rear of the train from Windsor under the District Line bridge. Beyond that is the bridge carrying Oxford Road. (R.E. Ruffell)

→ 42. 4SUB no. 4659 is seen from Oxford Road on 18th October 1973, having circumnavigated the Kingston loop or "gorn rand the owses". Apart from raising the platforms and the introduction of class 455 sliding-door stock, little has changed. (J. Scrace)

PUTNEY

41. A station was provided when the line opened but in 1885-86 it was totally rebuilt while the tracks were being quadrupled. Buses on routes 14, 4 and 52 are represented in this view from the straw boater era. The station exterior and the adjacent buildings are little changed today. (Lens of Sutton)

BARNES

43. The most imposing building on the route survives in 1988 basically unchanged. The varied chimney stacks compare favourably with Hampton Court Palace. The road bridge and canopy were altered after the 1886 quadrupling. (Lens of Sutton)

VI. The map is from 1913 and includes the goods yards, which closed in 1969, and all four signal boxes.

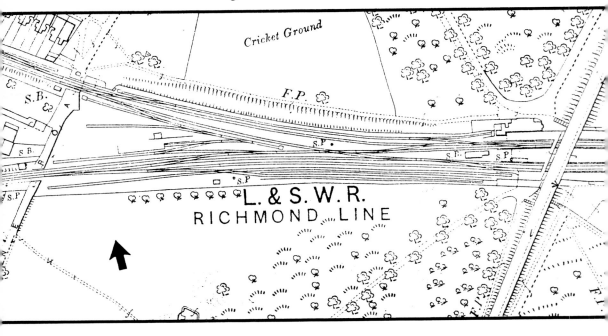

South Western Ry.

BARNES

S.2   **TO**

KINGSTON

Fare 1/3   3rd Class

4381

L B & S.C. & L & S.W
ONE SHILLING DAY
CRYSTAL PALACE
Including admission
TO   S.1
BARNES
Via Clapham Junc
See   1st Class
over   Fare 3/4
L & S.W. & L.B. & S.C.
ONE SHILLING DAY
BARNES
S.1   **TO**
CRYSTAL PALACE
Including admission
Via Clapham Junc
1st Class
Fare 3/4

9279

44. Apart from modernisation of the lighting, this charming view from Barnes Common is little altered today and well worth interrupting a journey to enjoy. An historic building, in country surroundings, so close to the city centre is quite unexpected. (Lens of Sutton)

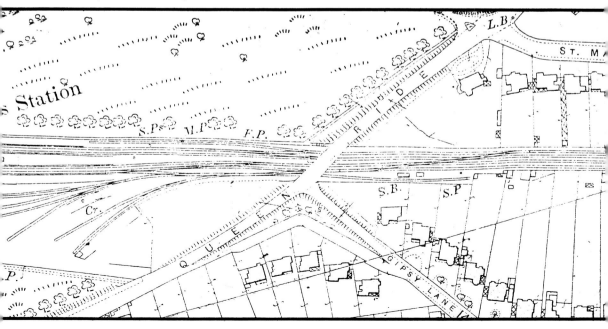

45. Looking west from the footbridge adjacent to the road bridge in September 1957, we see the Hounslow lines diverging to the right and Barnes Junction Box. East Box is behind us – see map – both closed on 22nd January 1959 when Barnes Panel Box came into use. It was erected to the right of the sub-station in the background. (D. Cullum)

46. A westward view between the up lines in 1961 shows a still complete station. Subsequently the canopy and buildings on the left were removed, as only the island is now normally used. The peace of Barnes Common was shattered on 2nd December 1955 when the 11.12 pm Waterloo to Windsor ran into the back of a freight train, under Queen's Ride bridge. There were 13 fatalities when fire took hold of the wooden coach bodies. (British Rail)

47. The fine chimneys are again evident on 25th March 1962 as class 02 no. 30199 takes the Railway Enthusiasts Club on a tour of South London. The small building to the left of the locomotive was used as a staff room and has subsequently been demolished. (S.C. Nash)

48. This box was provided to control the level crossing and another was provided only yards further north, on the loop line. Both were replaced by full lifting barriers in 1976. Two schemes were drawn up in 1901 for a curved connection between the two lines. One involved a flyover and the other showed two platforms on the spur. (J. Scrace)

49. The next crossing is ½ mile west and, from June 1974, the box only controlled the gates. The lane had nothing to do with football at all. In December 1976, the gates were replaced by barriers supervised under CCTV from Barnes Panel. (C. Hall)

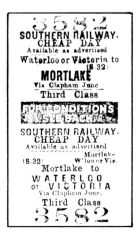

SOUTHERN RLY.
Mortlake to
WINDSOR & ETON
by Rail Third Class,
thence by Salter Bro's
Steamer Windsor to
CLEVEDON WOODS or
COOKHAM
0228

→ 51. A view at 90° to the previous one gives an impression of the heavy road traffic in Sheen Lane that the signalman had to intercept with his gates. An 1896 plan shows a royal waiting room on the station – maybe it was used by visitors to the nearby Richmond Park.
(Lens of Sutton)

MORTLAKE

50. Trains called here from the outset but the covered footbridge was a later addition. An M7 heads an up Reading train, delaying milk delivery in the pre-bottle age. (Lens of Sutton)

52. Adams 4–4–2T no.0429 approaches Mortlake with a special down coal train. The dull conductor rail and clean insulators suggests a date of 1916. The headcode is "Special Nine Elms – Windsor via Twickenham". (D. Cullum collection)

53. This and the previous picture are reminders that urban lineside allotments were much in demand. With the station in the background, class F1 no.1204 accelerates towards Barnes, with a fine clear exhaust. (D. Cullum collection)

54. Few differences were noticeable in 1988, apart from the updated lighting and name boards. The gates gave way to two lifting barriers in 1974 but these were replaced by the more usual four, in 1980. CCTV is now installed. (Lens of Sutton)

NORTH SHEEN

55. The steady expansion of London justified the opening of a new station on 6th July 1930. The tracks were slewed apart and an island platform built, access to which was via a concrete footbridge, seen in the background. The new SR style illuminated nameboard and lettered light globes were provided. (Lens of Sutton)

56. A Windsor bound class 455 unit glides between the allotments and the footpath to the station on 16th August 1987. In 1988, the half-hourly trains to Kingston called here, the former Hounslow and Kingston loop services having been withdrawn. (J. Scrace)

57. Known as Black Horse Crossing until September 1931, the box controlled gates over Manor Road until 1976, when barriers and CCTV were installed. (J. Scrace)

VII. The 1933 edition shows the branch to Kew Gardens diverging with the gas works siding parallel. The separate siding was to Hazelby's timber yard.

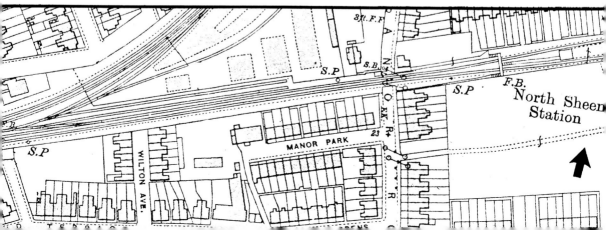

RICHMOND

58. This was part of the confusing scene that was presented to passengers until the stations were rebuilt in 1936. There were two entrances, between Kew Road and Parkshot, to the main line platforms and a separate approach road to "New Station", the 1869 terminus. (J. Pitt collection)

VIII. The 1864 survey shows, top right, points laid ready for the Hammersmith branch. Before this opened on 1st January 1869, a new terminus was built – see next map. The original terminus is marked "Goods Station" and was in use from July 1846 until August 1848.

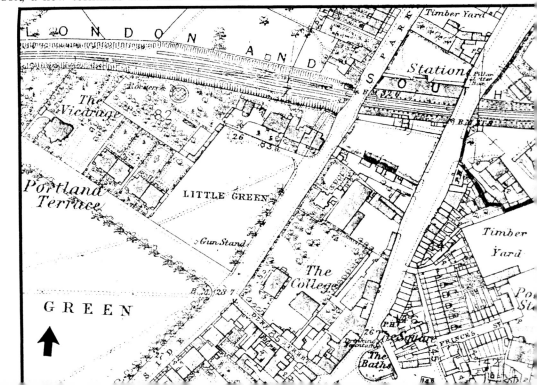

59. A down train from Waterloo passes under Church Road, with all six signals "off". The entrance to the goods yard is to the right of the locomotive and the terminal platforms are on the left. The through platforms were extended to the bridge in November 1936. (Lens of Sutton)

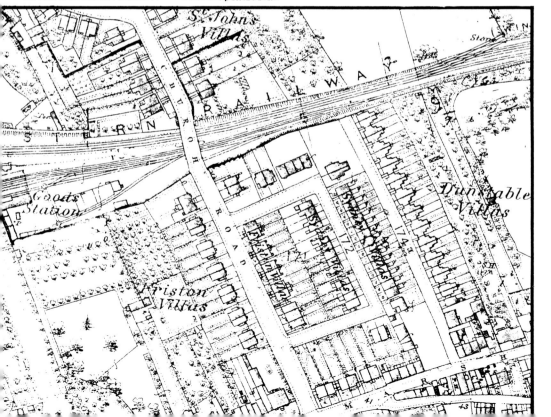

60. The original terminus remained in use for goods until 1936, when a new yard and shed came into use, north-east of the station. Royalty featured in Richmond's pre-railway history – a notable event was the death of Queen Elizabeth I in the town. (Lens of Sutton)

61. A photograph from Church Road shows conductor rails in the terminal platforms but not on the through lines. The District line was electrified in 1904 and the Kingston route in 1916. The locomotive on the right is class T1 no.75 and the train on the left is from Kingston. (D. Cullum collection)

IX. The 1933 edition reveals a footpath running between the stations. Two signal boxes are shown – West Box closed and Junction Box was replaced by a new one on 28th January 1940. The siding on the right passes into the corporation depot, where two wagons could be accommodated inside the gate. This map is almost continuous with that shown for North Sheen.

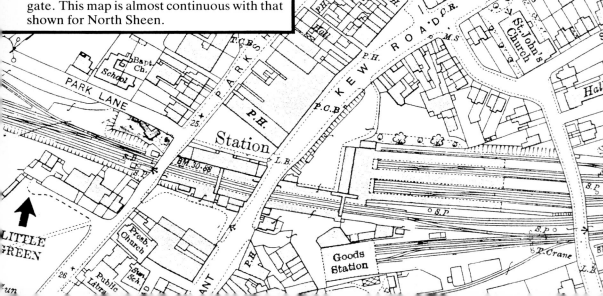

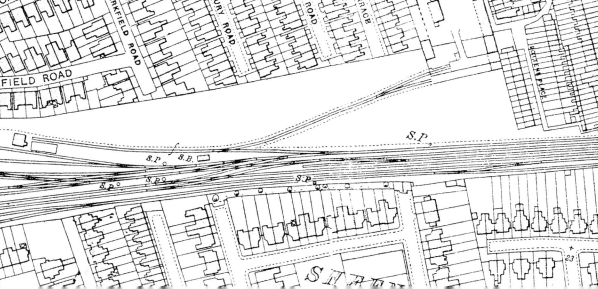

62. Looking from the down Waterloo platform (no.1) on 16th June 1987, we witness the departure of the 13.35 to North Woolwich via the North London Line. Until May 1985, trains on this route terminated at Broad Street. Obscured by the leading coach is the 1940 signal box, which since November 1970 has only controlled trains on the Kew Gardens line. The connection in the middle of the picture was laid in 1974 and platform 3 became a bay for Southern Region parcels traffic only. The connection to the left was restored in 1985, so that North London trains could use nos.3 and 4. It also gave a necessary link to enable stock to reach Selhurst Depot for servicing. LT trains have subsequently used three platforms – 5, 6 and 7. (J. Scrace)

63. One of the major engineering structures on the route is Richmond Bridge over the tidal Thames. It received an unusual load on 3rd April 1966, as U class no. 31639 and N class 31411 make their last run on BR, with a LCGB railtour from Waterloo via Twickenham, Hounslow, Clapham Junction, Herne Hill, Redhill, Reading, Southampton and Woking. (J. Scrace)

ST. MARGARETS

64. High class residential development had advanced sufficiently to justify opening a station on 2nd October 1876. This rural view shows one of Mr. Adam's square spectacled locomotives descending from Richmond Bridge, ½ mile distant, with a Windsor train. (Lens of Sutton)

65. Track men were still allowed to cover sleepers with ballast when this early photograph of the up side building was taken. Lattice and timber signal posts contrast in this and the next view. (Lens of Sutton)

66. Class 415 no. 490 discharges spare steam as its coaches discharge passengers from the city. The up relief line on the left was brought into use from Twickenham on 26th November 1899. The perforated signal sighting boards seldom appear in detail in photographs. (Lens of Sutton)

X. The 1896 survey, before 'semis' spread all round the railway.

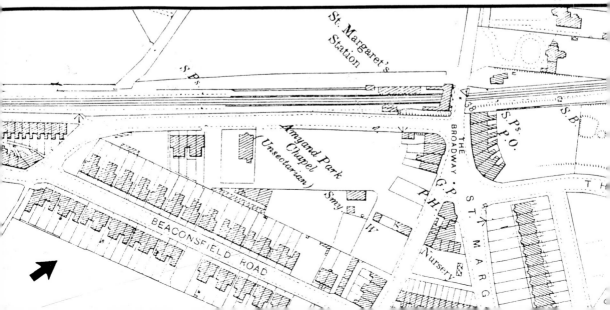

67. The up relief line came to an end opposite St. Margarets Box, which closed in November 1974. The trap points and sand drag were added in 1938, no doubt as a result of an accident elsewhere. (D. Cullum)

TWICKENHAM

68. The spaciousness of the station approach contrasted with cramped buildings and platforms, which became particularly congested in peak hours in their latter years. (Lens of Sutton)

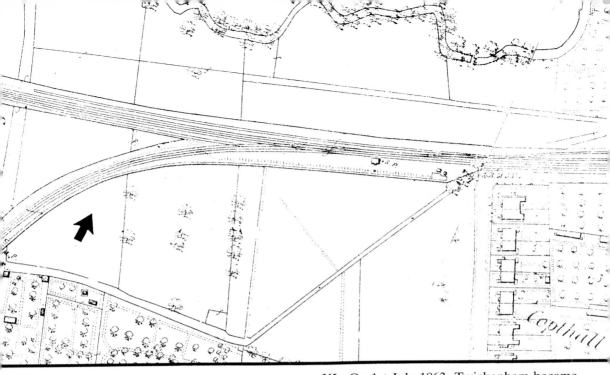

69. Top hat and tails contrast with the boaters of the humble clerks as an up train enters the island platform. A roofless extension to the footbridge is evident, on the right. (Lens of Sutton)

XI. On 1st July 1863, Twickenham became the junction for the Kingston branch but this map of 1864 does not show any signal boxes – simply cabins by the two signal posts. The engine shed, by the turntable, closed in 1897. Note the extensive orchards – Poupart's jam factory was built nearby.

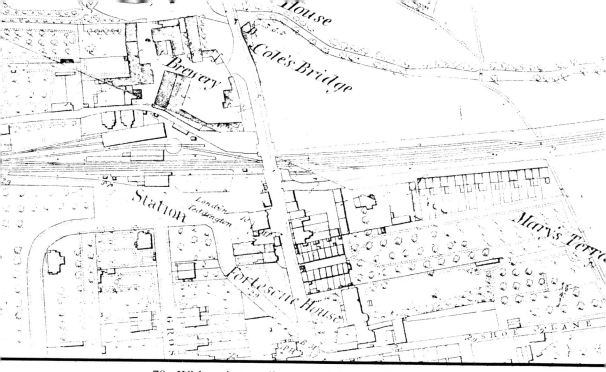

70. With paint peeling and slates missing, the station building nears the end of its life. The strip of granite setts is a reminder of the days when the rest of the station yard was loose gravel. Work on a new station was delayed by WWII and the years of difficulty that followed. (J. Pitt)

71. A photograph from the down platform shows the new station, beyond London Road bridge, a week before it was brought into use on 28th March 1954. The platform edge and canopy on the right had been cut back and the track slewed when work started before WWII. (D. Cullum)

73. No time was lost in destroying the dilapidated station which had lingered on for fifteen years, in a dreadful condition. U class 2–6–0 no. 31612 passes through with a return football excursion, bound for Lydney (Monmouthshire) on 17th April 1954. (S.C. Nash)

72. A glimpse of the down end on the same day shows the flyover in the mist and West Box, which had replaced an adjacent one on 19th January 1947. The sidings on the right remained in use until 1980. (D. Cullum)

74. As many as 20 extra trains would be run on Saturdays for the benefit of visitors to the nearby – fairly nearby – rugby football ground. Two bay platforms were provided in the new station for this traffic but on 20th August 1969, platform 1 was occupied by *Flying Scotsman*, with its American exhibition train. (R.E. Ruffell)

XII. The LSWR was one of the pioneers of flyovers and burrowing junctions and this was one of their first flyovers, being completed in 1882. The up platform became an island and was lengthened at this time. On the left of this 1934 edition is a gated siding to

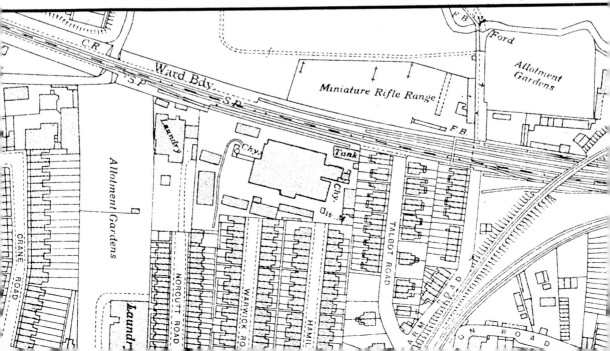

the works of the Twickenham & Teddington Electric Supply Co., which ceased to receive rail traffic in June 1938. This page can be rolled slightly to link with the map on the page after next.

75. The earlier East Box closed in June 1938. This temporary structure (and West Box) closed on 10th November 1974, six months after this photograph was taken. To ease football traffic congestion after WWII, a temporary wooden-faced ash-covered platform was in use for departing up trains only. It was on the site of the present platform 3. (J. Scrace)

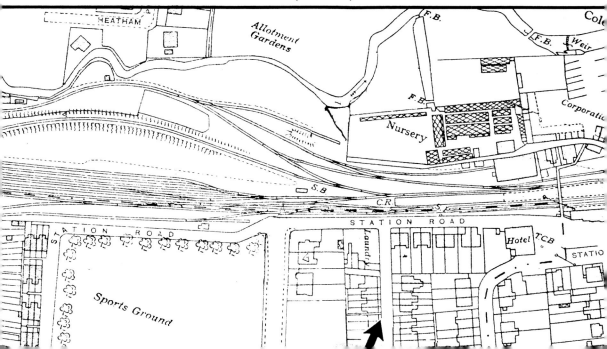

76. Having passed under the flyover in the background, no. 47638 conveys empty stock to Stewarts Lane Depot for servicing, on 18th June 1987. The train had formed the 8.20 Nottingham to Ascot race special and is passing over the site of the original island platform. (J. Scrace)

77. The tiny Kneller Box, which closed in July 1973, was named after Sir Godfrey Kneller's home, Kneller Hall, which now houses the Royal Military School of Music. Relief signalmen might have preferred to have been sent here than to Reformatory Box, with its implications. That was a small box, beyond Feltham, near H.M. Remand Centre. It was demolished in 1965. (J. Scrace)

2nd · SINGLE

Twickenham To

WHITTON

0143   0143

(S) 2½d. FARE 2½d. (S)

For conditions see over

XII. Continuation of the main map shows the goods yard, in 1934, and the site for the new station. The yard closed on 2nd January 1967. Tram tracks are shown in London Road for route 67, which became trolleybus route 667 in 1935 and is now bus 267.

WHITTON

78. An up train from the Hounslow loop calls on 12th September 1973. This service called at all stations to Waterloo while the Windsor/Weybridge trains gave a fast service. This dormitory station has steel canopies and pre-cast concrete components for almost everything else. It was opened on 6th July 1930. (J. Scrace)

79. Whitton Junction forms the south-east corner of the triangular junction with the Hounslow loop. The spur was opened on 1st January 1883 and since May 1987 has only been used by a few weekday peak services. This and the three Feltham boxes closed on 8th September 1974, when Feltham Panel came into use. (J. Scrace)

FELTHAM JUNCTION

80. This is the south-west corner of the triangular junction and has always handled a high proportion of freight services, particularly to and from the Midland and Northern lines via Acton and Willesden Junction.
(Lens of Sutton)

81. The box at the junction closed in October 1921 when this one came into use. It was further west and controlled the access to the London end of the new Feltham marshalling yard, by way of the line on the right.
(J. Scrace)

FELTHAM MARSHALLING YARD

Approximately in the centre of the area an office building has been erected, providing, on the ground floor, guards' and shunters' rooms and the offices of the yardmaster and his clerk. Above is a telephone exchange connecting with all parts of the yard and in communication with the official telephone system serving the London & South Western Railway system, and a conference room where periodical conferences are held by representatives of the goods and traffic departments. The building is surmounted by a clock tower having four clock faces, about 6 ft. in diameter, and visible from all parts of the yard. These clocks are electrically operated, using the Synchronome Company's mechanism, and are controlled by a master clock in the telephone room, which also operates all other clocks in the offices, signal cabins and about the yard. Towards Feltham station a lawn and shrubbery is being laid out on a piece of land not otherwise occupied, while on the other side of the office building is a battery and motor generator house for supplying electric current for the signal cabins, point mechanisms and track circuits.

82. A contemporary photograph and report gives an excellent impression of the new offices (Railway Gazette)

83. The yard was one mile long and is seen here from the west end, not long before its completion. The up reception sidings are under construction, behind Feltham East Box. (Lens of Sutton)

Opened in stages during 1921-22, it was then the most up to date mechanised yard in the country. It took over shunting work previously performed at Nine Elms, Brentford and Woking on the LSWR system and at Willesden (LNWR) and Brent (MR). These last two yards had previously made up trains to Nine Elms, Woking, Basingstoke, Southampton and Wimbledon.

There was a considerable reduction in goods train mileage, not only from the concentration on Feltham but also because the long departure and reception sidings and lengthy block sections to the south-west enabled much longer trains to be run.

Apart from some long distance express departures in the evening, the working of Nine Elms traffic to Feltham via the Windsor lines avoided the complicated crossing of the main lines at Queens Road West and gave a reduction in the number of goods movements between Nine Elms and Weybridge.

Summary of arrivals and departures during the winter of 1938-39

Down Departures to –		Down Arrivals from –		Up Departures to –		Up Arrivals from –	
Southampton	5	Brent	10	Brent	10	Southampton	2
Bournemouth	1	Neasden	3	Neasden	3	Bournemouth	1
Reading	3	Willesden	8	Willesden	8	Reading	3
Datchet/Windsor	2	Ferme Pk/East Goods	8	Ferme Pk	8	Datchet/Windsor	2
Wimbledon	3	Nine Elms	5	Hither Green	3	Wimbledon	2
Woking	3	Hither Green	3	Nine Elms	6	Woking	1
Eastleigh	1	Plumstead	1	Locals	7	Eastleigh	3
Exmouth Jct	1	Battersea Yard	1		45	Fratton via Eastleigh	1
Farnham	1	Locals	6			Farnham	1
Addlestone	1		45			Bevois Park	2
Surbiton	1					Walton	1
	22					Guildford	1
						Basingstoke	1
						Haslemere	1
						Ashford (Middx)	1
						Sunningdale	1
							45

XIII. 1948 control diagram. The River Crane and two other waterways had to be covered before construction could commence. Cattle pens were provided to facilitate the feeding and watering of animals in transit. In 1988, the entire site was derelict, the clock tower and offices a ghostly shell.

Feltham Marshalling Yard consists of 32 miles of Sidings, embracing 73 roads, and is worked on the gravitation principle of having one "Hump" in the Down Yard and one "Hump" in the Up Yard.

Down Yard trains are mainly received from other Regions via the following junctions :—

Eastern Region	G.C. Section	Via Neasden, Kew and Hounslow;
	G.N. Section	Metropolitan Lines, Blackfriars Bridge and Barnes ;
	G.E. Section	Temple Mills, Willesden, Kew and Hounslow ;
London Midland Region	N.W. Section	Willesden, Kew and Hounslow ;
	Midland Section	Brent, Kew and Hounslow ;

and from the Southern Region (London East Division) via Clapham Junction.

Up Yard trains are received from the South-West and West of England via Chertsey, and from the Western Region via Reading. Local Suburban Services work into both Yards.

Approximately 68 trains arrive and 73 depart every 24 hours, and additional special trains as required.

There are eight Up Reception Sidings capable of holding trains of 60 wagons each, and there are ten Down Reception Sidings.

From the Reception Sidings wagons are shunted over a hump to a series of tracks on the opposite side which spread out fanwise from the foot of the hump.

The movement of trains towards the humps is controlled by signals which can be operated either from the hump boxes or by Shunter from ground level. These signals work in conjunction with a "Klaxon" horn which is situated half way in the Reception sidings. The sounding of the horn warns the Driver of the Hump shunting engine by a code of hoots as to the position of the signal, whether in the "On" or "Off". In order to assist generally the working of the Reception sidings, a loudspeaker unit is installed in both hump boxes which permits verbal instructions to be given by the Hump Pointsman to Drivers of incoming trains or Shunters.

Moving very steadily the engine pushes the train of wagons to be split up at about 2 m.p.h. up the hump. The Leading Shunter on the hump uncouples the wagons and chalks on the first wagon the number of the road to which it is to run, and this is observed by the Hump Box Pointsman, who sets the road by pressing the buttons so required on his diagrammatic board. As this wagon passes him he observes the number chalked on its rear end, and this tells him which road is required for the next shunt. In fact, after the first wagon has been dealt with the Pointsman does not require to pay any attention to the train which is being shunted, but only to observe the number chalked on each wagon as it passes him and to set the road accordingly as soon as it clears the points. A powerful electric lamp is provided at one corner of the Signal Box so that the numbers in chalk can be seen after dark, its rays being directed to show them up at the most convenient position for observation. In the War years, the numbers had to be announced to the Pointsman over a Loudaphone by a man on the ground, which method is also used during dense fog. The Hump Boxes are electrically controlled and have been designed to suit conditions at Feltham.

The Up hump provides access to 18 Marshalling Sidings from which goods trains depart for other Regions and for local stations to London.

The Down hump leads to 20 Marshalling Sidings from which departure is made for points in West and South-West England, also Suburban stations via Chertsey.

The normal average day turnover is 2,750 wagons in and 2,750 wagons out. These figures do not include transfers from Up to Down Yard and vice versa, or internal working. During ideal conditions, some 7,000 wagons have been dealt with in one day during War period.

In the centre between Up and Down Yards are cattle pens for feeding and watering cattle in transit, a Dock for transhipping loads from defective wagons, a large wagon Repair Depot and an Office.

84. A down special train behind class M7 no. 30241 passes the yard on 8th May 1954. The coaches are probably empties destined for Walton-on-Thames. On the skyline, above East Box, is the observation and clock tower and on the right is the silhouette of the locomotive coaling hopper. (C.R.L. Coles)

85. Two humps were provided with gradients of 1 in 140 up and 1 in 50 down, which was followed by a length of 1 in 150 before reaching the level marshalling area. Class G16 4-8-0Ts were designed for this work – no. 30495 is seen having propelled a freight train over the down hump. The brake van is running away from the engine. (C.R.L. Coles)

86. One of the powerful class 9F 2-10-0s arrived on test on 24th April 1957 and is seen on the 65ft. turntable, with its vacuum brake pipe supplying power to turn the table. On the right is the down hump signal box, from where the marshalling siding points were set electrically in accordance with the siding number previously chalked onto the ends of the wagons. (D. Cullum)

87. Up to 80 locomotives were allocated here and the shed could house over 40 tender engines. For many years all the class H16 4–6–2Ts (used on transfer trips to other yards) were based here, as were all the class G16 4–8–0Ts. Taken on 10th March 1964, this photograph shows W class no. 31912 at the west end – a repair road at the other end was provided with a 50-ton overhead crane. (J. Scrace)

88. Diesels first appeared in the yard in 1954 and with the end of steam scheduled for July 1967, a diesel depot was built where the coal stacks formerly stood. This view is from August 1968 – the yard closed on 6th January 1969. Marshalling yards flourish in mainland Europe – maybe a more sensible national transport policy will be forthcoming when BR is connected to it. (R.E. Ruffell)

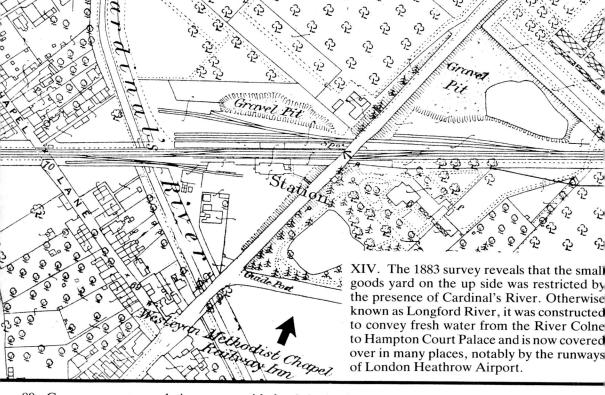

XIV. The 1883 survey reveals that the small goods yard on the up side was restricted by the presence of Cardinal's River. Otherwise known as Longford River, it was constructed to convey fresh water from the River Colne to Hampton Court Palace and is now covered over in many places, notably by the runways of London Heathrow Airport.

89. Generous accommodation was provided at an early date at this station, which, like Ashford and Staines, was opened with the line. By the time this postcard was produced, it had a footbridge but the up bay platform was used as a goods siding. The train originated at Windsor. (Lens of Sutton)

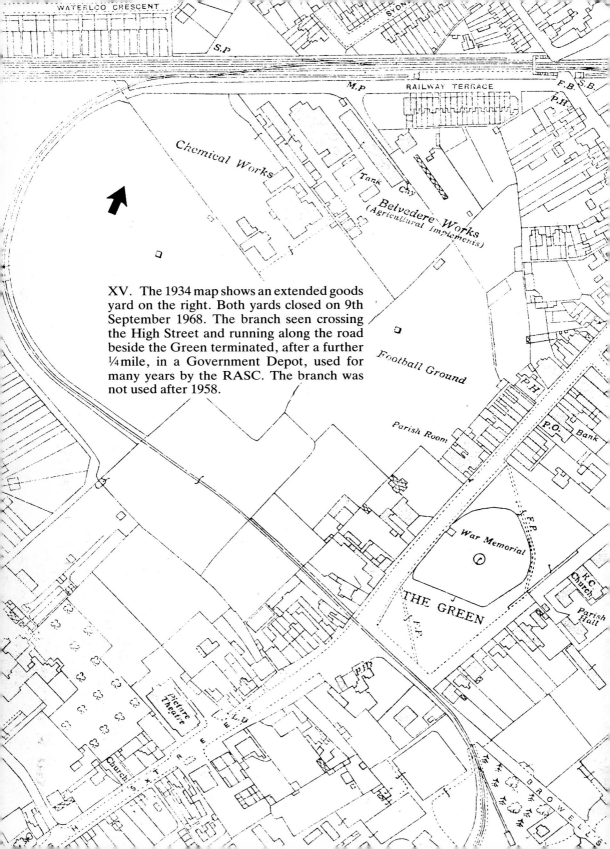

WATERLOO CRESCENT

SYDN

S.P.

M.P RAILWAY TERRACE F.B. S.B.

P.H.

Chemical Works

Tank Chy

Belvedere Works
(Agricultural Implements)

XV. The 1934 map shows an extended goods yard on the right. Both yards closed on 9th September 1968. The branch seen crossing the High Street and running along the road beside the Green terminated, after a further ¼ mile, in a Government Depot, used for many years by the RASC. The branch was not used after 1958.

Football Ground

P.H.

P.O. Bank

Parish Room

F.P.

War Memorial

R.C. Church

THE GREEN

Parish Hall

F.P.

P.H.

Picture Theatre

L.U.

B R O W E L L

Church

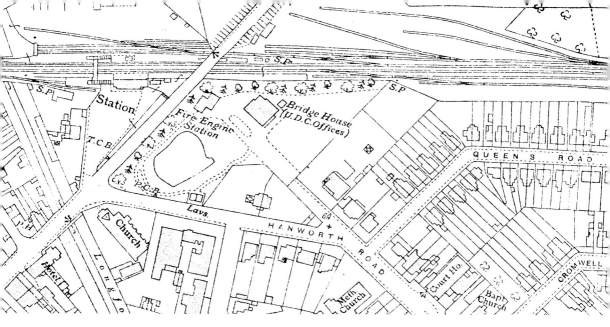

90. The river passes under the line in front of the locomotive, which appears to be running round its train. West Box controls the Bedfont Lane crossing and East Box peeps up behind the Hounslow Road bridge. This box was replaced in October 1921 by the one seen in photograph nos. 83 and 84. Steps up to the main road can be seen between the station and the goods shed. (Lens of Sutton)

91. A Reading bound train, headed by class T1 0–4–4 no. 76 passes under the footbridge which the SR replaced by a covered concrete one, near to the road bridge. (Lens of Sutton)

92. Associated with the new footbridge was a new station entrance and booking office, close to the car on the right. This has proved to be a traffic hazard and as the road is in need of widening, they are to be demolished and this fine Victorian building is to be brought back into use. (Lens of Sutton)

93. Apart from the loss of the semaphore signal and West Box, little has altered since they were photographed in August 1974. In 1988, just one siding remained usable. It was on the down side, beyond the road bridge and opposite the Feltham Panel Box. (J. Scrace)

XVI. ½ mile west of Feltham (pronounced Felt-ham), private sidings were provided for Boyers and A.W. Smith. This is Boyer's system in 1914, with lines shown both sides of the massive glasshouses and one continuing, apparently through an engine shed, to Feltham Farm. This was at Lower Feltham. The area is now covered with houses but some of the roads follow the line of the former railway. Scale 15″ to 1 mile.

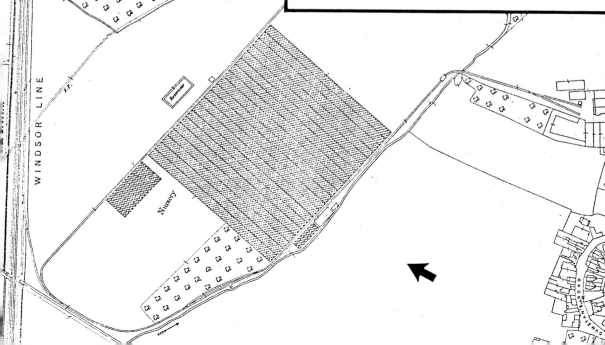

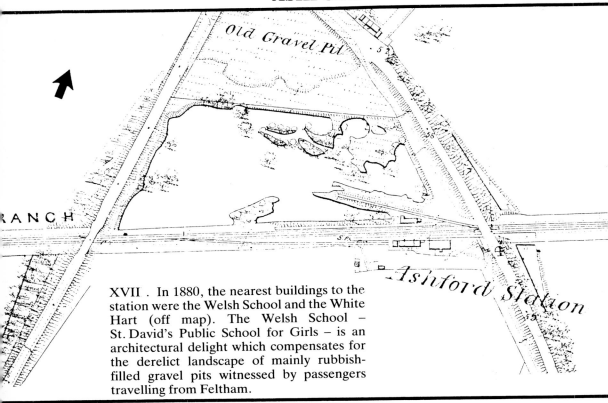

XVII . In 1880, the nearest buildings to the station were the Welsh School and the White Hart (off map). The Welsh School – St. David's Public School for Girls – is an architectural delight which compensates for the derelict landscape of mainly rubbish-filled gravel pits witnessed by passengers travelling from Feltham.

94. The up platform is still equally crowded on weekday mornings but the goods shed has gone (closed in 1965) and the shelter has been replaced by a fully glazed one. (Lens of Sutton)

95. The box, partially obscured by steam in the previous picture, was demolished in 1930 to permit platform lengthening. This is its replacement, which was on the down side and was made redundant by the Feltham Panel in 1974. (J. Scrace)

XVIII. The 1934 edition shows the goods yards at their fullest extent.

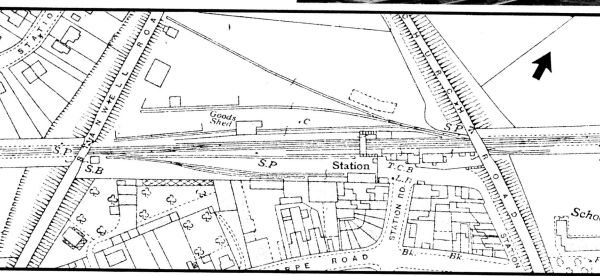

96. The down side has changed little over the years, retaining its small brick building although the station house has been rendered and painted white. The gas lights and enamelled signs have disappeared. (Lens of Sutton)

STAINES

97. Originally simply "Staines", it was known as "Staines Junction" from 1885 until January 1923, when it became "Staines Central". The suffix was dropped on 18th January 1966. An up Windsor train approaches, in an early undated postcard view. (Lens of Sutton)

98. Class A12 no. E618 takes the left hand track, with a train to Reading on 16th January 1927. The Windsor line curves right beside two sidings which remained in use until 1975. (H.C. Casserley)

99. An early morning up train takes the curve from the Virginia Water line on 9th April 1969, passing the West Yard which is busy with steel and container traffic. One of the two sidings on the right is electrified for use as a carriage siding. (R.E. Ruffell)

London & South Western Ry.
This Ticket is issued subject to the By-laws,
Regulations & Conditions stated in the
Company's Time Tables Bills & Notices
STAINES JUNC to
TWICKENHAM
Staines   Staines
Twickenham   Twickenham
1st CLASS   1st CLASS
Fare 1/7   Fare 1/7
O14

SOUTHERN RAILWAY.
Issued subject to the Bye-laws, Regulations &
Conditions in the Company's Bills and Notices.
Windsor & Eton   to
Windsor & Eton   Windsor & Eton
Staines   Staines
STAINES
THIRD CLASS   THIRD CLASS
Fare 1/1   Fare 1/1
NOT TRANSFERABLE.
3900

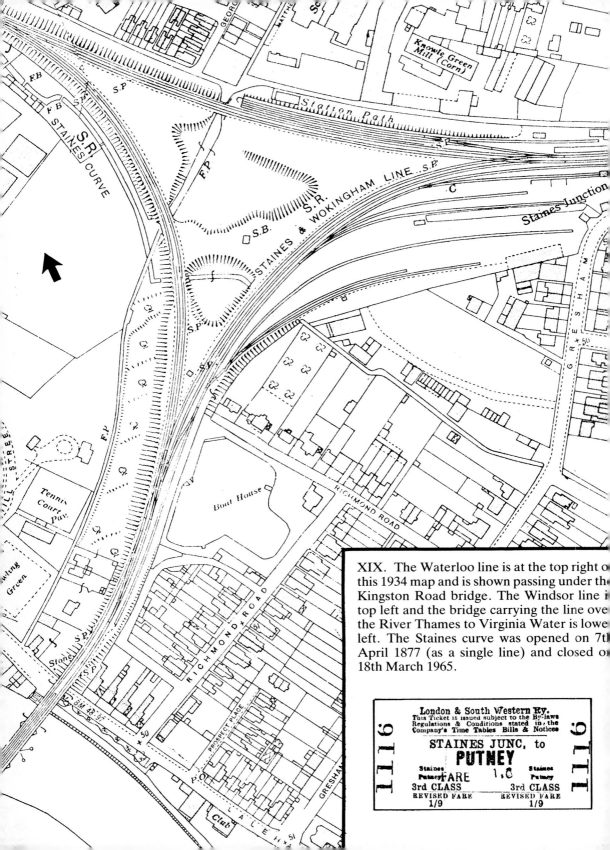

XIX. The Waterloo line is at the top right o[f] this 1934 map and is shown passing under the Kingston Road bridge. The Windsor line i[s] top left and the bridge carrying the line ove[r] the River Thames to Virginia Water is lowe[r] left. The Staines curve was opened on 7t[h] April 1877 (as a single line) and closed o[n] 18th March 1965.

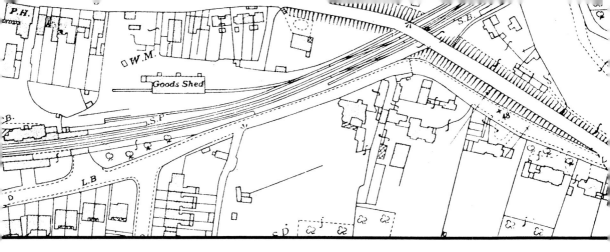

100. This box was on the down side, east of the Kingston Road bridge, and was in use from 1930 until September 1974. It replaced two electro-pneumatic boxes – East, which was quite close to it, and West, which was in the triangle. These had been brought into use in 1904, replacing five earlier boxes. (J. Scrace)

SOUTHERN RAILWAY.
This Ticket is issued subject to the By-laws
Regulations & Conditions stated in the
Company's Time Tables Bills & Notices
Available on day of issue only
WINDSOR & ETON to
TWICKENHAM
Windsor & E.   Windsor & E
Twickenham   Twickenham
3rd CLASS   3rd CLASS
Fare 1/9   Fare 1/9

9437   9437

101. The handsome exterior was similar but superior to Feltham's. The warm yellow brick is in contrast to the red structure with steel faced canopy erected by the SR on the down side. (C. Hall)

102. The all timber goods shed surprisingly survived in 1988, although the sidings here and in East Yard had ceased to be used by 1973. Four of the sidings were relaid and electrified in 1974, for carriage berthing. (C. Hall)

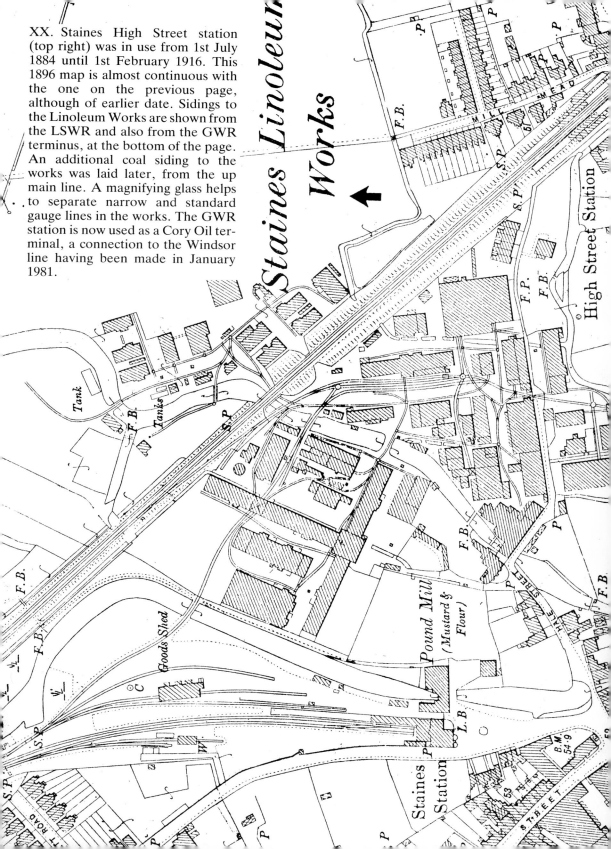

XX. Staines High Street station (top right) was in use from 1st July 1884 until 1st February 1916. This 1896 map is almost continuous with the one on the previous page, although of earlier date. Sidings to the Linoleum Works are shown from the LSWR and also from the GWR terminus, at the bottom of the page. An additional coal siding to the works was laid later, from the up main line. A magnifying glass helps to separate narrow and standard gauge lines in the works. The GWR station is now used as a Cory Oil terminal, a connection to the Windsor line having been made in January 1981.

Staines Linoleum Works

High Street Station

Tank

Tanks

F.B.

S.P.

Goods Shed

F.B.

Pound Mill (Mustard & Flour)

Staines Station

Pound Mill

L.B.

F.B.

B.M. 54·9

53

STREET

HALE STREET

103. The LCGB "South Western Suburban Railtour" returns from Windsor and crosses Staines Moor on 5th February 1967, behind no. 34100 *Appledore*. It is viewed from the former GWR Staines West branch, which carried passengers from 1885 until 1965. A connection between the SR and the GWR was laid during WWII, to give an alternative route in the event of wartime emergencies. (S.C. Nash)

XXI. 1988 diagram. Dotted lines show tracks lifted.
A. Ex-GWR branch, closed to freight on 28th January 1981.
B. Connection available for use between 23rd June 1940 and 16th December 1947.
C. Spur brought into use on 28th January 1981.
D. West Curve 1877 - 1965.

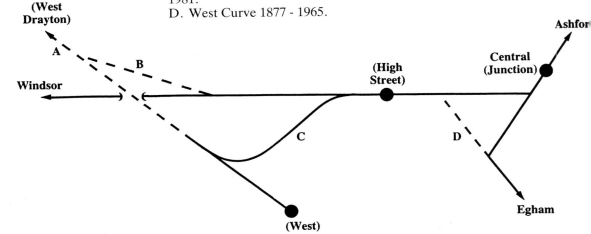

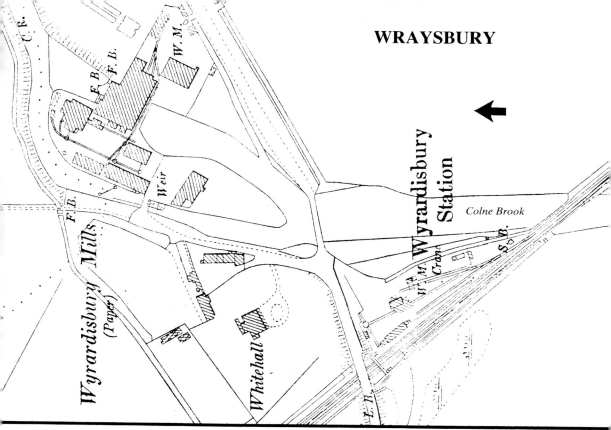

Colne Brook

104. The station came into use when the line opened, but the platforms were beyond the road bridge until about 1860. Two horse boxes stand by the up starting signal as a train approaches from Windsor. The goods shed is beyond the loading gauge. (Lens of Sutton)

XXII. The 1896 edition shows the earlier form of spelling, not then used by the railway, and a narrow gauge system at the mill. Sidings were later provided on the up side, for Boyers, and on the down for the Wraysbury Sand & Gravel Co.

105. A similar view in October 1965, taken from the bridge over Colne Brook, shows that all the sidings had been lifted (the yard closed in 1962) but that the signal box retained its nameboard although it had been closed seven months earlier. All the buildings have since been demolished. (D. Cullum)

SUNNYMEADS

106. This island platform was brought into use on 10th July 1927, mainly to serve some Thames-side dwellings. Looking towards Windsor, we see the booking office on the left, which is no longer in use. To the west of the station, Remenham siding once served a nearby gravel pit – one of a number in the area now worked out. (Lens of Sutton)

107. The up side buildings have been incorporated into a row of four shops and although the wooden goods shed, seen beyond the house, was not included, at least the station survives, despite a serious fire in September 1986. In 1988, the booking office was in use on weekday mornings. (Lens of Sutton)

108. The High Street level crossing is shown in April 1968 – five years later the gates were replaced by full lifting barriers. The box ceased to function in December 1974, its duties having been transferred to Feltham. (J. Scrace)

109. No. 73129 draws level with the station house on 7th August 1974, with a special royal train to Southampton Docks. No. 73123 is at the rear, as reversal would be necessary with the loss of the Staines West curve. (J. Scrace)

XXIII. The 1899 survey indicates the proximity of the station to the village centre.

110. The location of Mays Crossing is shown on the map. Manpower costs were reduced on 17th December 1974, by the transfer of control of lifting barriers to Feltham Panel, under CCTV. (J. Scrace)

111. One mile west of Datchet, the line crosses the River Thames and enters the northern part of Home Park, effectively the "front garden" of Windsor Castle. The train is the LCGB Railtour, previously seen at Staines Moor in the last year of Southern Region steam. (J. Scrace)

WINDSOR and ETON RIVERSIDE

XXIV. The proximity of the river and the castle is evident in this 1899 survey – the castle rampart commences in the lower left part of the map.

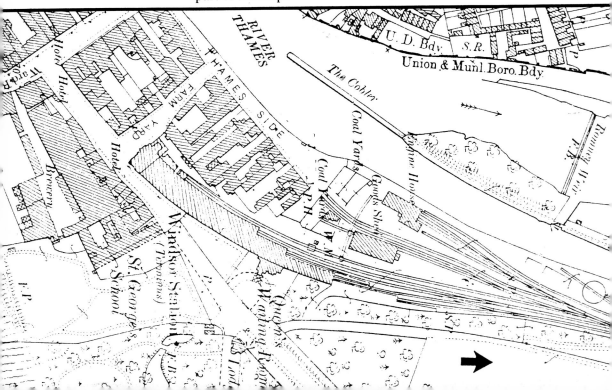

112. With Windsor Castle in the background, class T9 4–4–0 no. E285 prepares for departure in about 1930. A 9-ton capacity crane stands near the entrance to the goods shed and a class M7 0–4–4T is seen beyond the loading gauge.
(D. Cullum collection)

113. The two-road locomotive shed is next to the water tank and partly hidden by coal staithes. It probably dated from the opening of the line and remained in partial use for several years after electrification.
(Lens of Sutton)

114. The wall on the right faces the castle and has in it a large number of double doors, for use on ceremonial occasions. Until 1930, there were scissors crossovers in the foreground. The 2NOL set seen here was typical of Windsor line services for over 25 years. This and the next photograph were taken on 1st December 1951. (D. Cullum)

115. Platform 1 had engine release facilities until 1965 after which time it was not possible to run round a train. This was remedied in 1975, when a crossover was laid between platforms 2 and 3. Goods facilities were withdrawn on 5th April 1965. (D. Cullum)